PRAYERS
FOR CHILDREN

Illustrated by
Eloise Wilkin

🪶 A GOLDEN BOOK · NEW YORK
Golden Books Publishing Company, Inc., New York, New York 10106

Acknowledgements

"A Great Gray Elephant" is reprinted with the permission of Simon & Schuster from *The Child on His Knees* by Mary Dixon Thayer. Copyright 1926 by Macmillan Publishing Company, copyright renewed 1954 by Mary D.T. Fremont-Smith.

Dear Father, Hear and Bless

Dear Father,
   hear and bless
Thy beasts
   and singing birds:
And guard
   with tenderness
Small things
   that have no words.

Morning Prayer

Now, before I run to play,
   Let me not forget to pray
To God Who kept me through the night
   And waked me with the morning light.

Help me, Lord, to love Thee more
   Than I ever loved before,
In my work and in my play,
   Be Thou with me through the day.

Amen.

I Thank Thee, Lord

I thank Thee, Lord, for quiet rest,
And for Thy care of me;
O let me through this day be blest
And kept from harm by Thee.

— Mary L. Duncan

The Gift

What can I give Him,
  Poor as I am?
If I were shepherd
  I would bring a lamb.
If I were a Wise Man
  I would do my part.
Yet what can I give Him?
  Give my heart.
        — Christina Rossetti

Be present at our table, Lord,
Be here and everywhere adored.
These morsels bless, and grant that we
May feast in Paradise with Thee. Amen.

A Great Gray Elephant

A great gray elephant,
   A little yellow bee,
   A tiny purple violet,
    A tall green tree,
A red and white sailboat
On a blue sea —
All these things
You gave to me,
When you made
My eyes to see —
   Thank you, God!

He Prayeth Well,
Who Loveth Well

He prayeth well
   Who loveth well
Both man and bird and beast.
He prayeth best
   Who loveth best
All things both great and small;
For the dear God
   Who loveth us,
He made and loveth all.

          —Samuel Taylor Coleridge,
           from *The Ancient Mariner*

Father, We Thank Thee

For flowers that bloom about our feet,
    Father, we thank Thee,
For tender grass so fresh and sweet,
    Father, we thank Thee,
For the song of bird and hum of bee,
For all things fair we hear or see,
Father in heaven, we thank Thee.

For blue of stream and blue of sky,
    Father, we thank Thee,
For pleasant shade of branches high,
    Father, we thank Thee,
For fragrant air and cooling breeze,
For beauty of the blooming trees,
Father in heaven, we thank Thee.

For this new morning with its light,
    Father, we thank Thee,
For rest and shelter of the night,
    Father, we thank Thee,
For health and food, for love and friends,
For everything Thy goodness sends,
Father in heaven, we thank Thee.

— Ralph Waldo Emerson

The Lord's Prayer

ur Father, Who art in heaven,
Hallowed be Thy Name.
Thy kingdom come,
Thy will be done,
In earth as it is in heaven.
Give us this day our daily bread,
And forgive us our debts,
As we forgive our debtors.
And lead us not into temptation
But deliver us from evil,
For thine is the kingdom,
And the power, and the glory,
Forever. Amen.

The Doxology

ise God, from whom all blessings flow;
ise Him, all creatures here below;
ise Him above, ye heavenly host:
ise Father, Son, and Holy Ghost. Amen.

Evening Hymn

I hear no voice, I feel no touch,
  I see no glory bright;
But yet I know that God is near,
  In darkness as in light.

He watches ever by my side,
  And hears my whispered prayer:
The Father for His little child
  Both night and day doth care.

— Anonymous

Jesus, Tender Shepherd, Hear Me

Jesus, tender Shepherd, hear me;
  Bless Thy little lamb tonight;
Through the darkness be Thou near me,
  Watch my sleep till morning light.

All this day Thy hand has led me,
  And I thank Thee for Thy care;
Thou has warmed and clothed and fed me;
  Listen to my evening prayer.

— Mary L. Duncan

A Child's Prayer

God, make my life a little light
  Within the world to glow;
A little flame that burneth bright
  Wherever I may go.

God, make my life a little flower
  That giveth joy to all,
Content to bloom in native bower,
  Although the place be small.

God, make my life a little song
  That comforteth the sad,
That helpeth others to be strong
  And makes the singer glad.

God, make my life a little staff
  Whereon the weak may rest,
And so what health and strength I have
  May serve my neighbors best.

God, make my life a little hymn
  Of tenderness and praise;
Of faith, that never waxeth dim,
  In all His wondrous ways.
                    — M. Betham-Edwards

Jesus, from Thy Throne on High

Jesus, from Thy throne on high,
    Far above the bright blue sky,
Look on me with loving eye;
    Hear me, Holy Jesus.

Be Thou with me every day,
    In my work and in my play,
When I learn and when I pray;
    Hear me, Holy Jesus.

— Thomas B. Pollock

A Good Way

Let's see, dear God, I want to tell
You in a brand new way
"I love you!" But I cannot think
Of anything to say.
I know, dear God! I'll run and do
Something for someone, and
Then when You see me doing it
Of course You'll understand!

— Mary Dixon Thayer

Good-Night Prayer

Father, unto Thee I pray,
Thou hast guarded me all day;
Safe I am while in Thy sight,
Safely let me sleep tonight.

Bless my friends, the whole world bless;
Help me to learn helpfulness;
Keep me ever in Thy sight;
So to all I say good night.

— Henry Johnstone

Bedtime Prayer

Now I lay me down to sleep,
I pray Thee, Lord, thy child to keep:
Thy love guard me through the night
And wake me with the morning light.
                                        Amen.

Good Night

Good night! Good night! Far flies the light;
But still God's love shall flame above,
Making all bright. Good night! Good night!

God Watches Us

od watches o'er us all the day, at home, at school, and at our play;
d when the sun has left the skies, he watches with a million eyes.

— Gabriel Setoun

Evening Prayer

Words adapted by Miriam Drury   *Miriam Drury*

Now I lay me down to sleep, I

pray Thee, Lord, Thy child to keep: Thy love guard me

through the night, And wake me with the morn-ing light.